You want to read this! This is your answer directly from the Word for questions you may have about the tumultuous times currently besieging our world. God is in control. Place your trust in him today!

Pastor Tim

END TIMES

AND THEN I SAW A NEW
HEAVEN AND A NEW EARTH . . .

REVELATION 21

TIM R. BARKER, D. MIN.

Tim R. Barker Ministries

END TIMES, Barker, Tim R.

ISBN: 978-1-7346669-4-6

END TIMES © 2020

TABLE OF CONTENTS

INTRODUCTION

The Book of Revelation and other prophetic books remind us that one day this life as we know it is coming to an end – whether it comes by way of death or the Lord's return – it will end.

In years past, we often heard sermons that were not simply pointing us to our final destination, rather they were our motivation in this life. Knowing that someday we will all stand before God serves as a powerful incentive to obey God completely and consistently.

Many have asked recently if the 2020

COVID-19 pandemic is prophetic and if I believe the end is near. My answer is yes and yes, because I am almost certain that this is all about to wrap up. Things are intensifying in unprecedented expedience, and I pray that we are all waiting in anticipation.

Scripture provides us a timeline of events that signal that the end is coming soon. Let me lead you through them.

THE CHURCH AGE

Romans 11:25, KJV: *"For I would not, brethren, that ye should be ignorant of this mystery, lest ye should be wise in your own conceits; that blindness in part is happened to Israel, until the fulness of the Gentiles be come in."*

The Church Age is the time period between Pentecost until the Rapture of the Church in which Gentiles are invited to participate in the blessings of the Abrahamic Covenant. During this time, God has extended to everyone to be a part of God's Kingdom by accepting His offer of salvation. Israel rejected Jesus but God has one final event in mind to turn the Israelites toward Himself and this is the Great Tribulation. However, before that final period of dealing with Israel can begin, another event must first occur.

THE RAPTURE OF THE CHURCH

1 Thessalonians 4:13-18, NIV: *"¹³ Brothers and sisters, we do not want you to be uninformed about those who sleep in death, so that you do not grieve like the rest of mankind, who have no hope. ¹⁴ For we believe that Jesus died and rose again, and so we believe that God will bring with Jesus those who have fallen asleep in him. ¹⁵ According to the Lord's word, we tell you that we who are still alive, who are left until the coming of the*

*Lord, will certainly not precede those
who have fallen asleep. ¹⁶ For the
Lord himself will come down from
heaven, with a loud command, with
the voice of the archangel and with
the trumpet call of God, and the dead
in Christ will rise first. ¹⁷ After that,
we who are still alive and are left will
be caught up together with them in
the clouds to meet the Lord in the air.
And so, we will be with the Lord
forever. ¹⁸ Therefore encourage one
another with these words."*

The Church Age is going to end with an
event that many refer to as the Rapture of
the Church. The word "rapture" comes from
a Greek word *harpazo* and it means "to
snatch away."

All Christians will be "snatched away"
just before the Tribulation period.

The Tribulation

Revelation, chapters 6-19, tells us that following the Rapture of the church will be a time referred to as the Great Tribulation. This is a seven-year period that will begin when the Antichrist signs a peace covenant with Israel and ends with Armageddon and the Second Coming of Jesus Christ.

The purpose of the Tribulation is two-fold: the salvation of both Jews and Gentiles and the judgment of unbelievers.

THE SECOND COMING OF JESUS CHRIST

Revelation 19:11-16, NIV: *"[11] I saw heaven standing open and there before me was a white horse, whose rider is called Faithful and True. With justice he judges and wages war. [12] His eyes are like blazing fire, and on his head are many crowns. He has a name written on him that no one knows but he himself. [13] He is dressed in a robe dipped in blood, and his name is the Word of God. [14] The armies of heaven were follow-*

ing him, riding on white horses and dressed in fine linen, white and clean. ¹⁵ Coming out of his mouth is a sharp sword with which to strike down the nations. He will rule them with an iron scepter. He treads the winepress of the fury of the wrath of God Almighty. ¹⁶ On his robe and on his thigh he has this name written: KING OF KINGS AND LORD OF LORDS."

The Second Coming of Christ is the visible return of Jesus Christ to establish His kingdom on earth. The climax of the Tribulation will occur during the war of Armageddon during which the major powers of the world will seek to defeat the Antichrist and his forces. But, as the world forces prepare to destroy one another, the heavens will suddenly open and all attention will be directed upward as the entire world watches the Second Coming of Jesus Christ.

THE MILLENNIUM

Revelation 20:1-3, NIV: *"And I saw an angel coming down out of heaven, having the key to the Abyss and holding in his hand a great chain. [2] He seized the dragon, that ancient serpent, who is the devil, or Satan, and bound him for a thousand years. [3] He threw him into the Abyss, and locked and sealed it over him, to keep him from deceiving the nations anymore until the thousand years were ended. After that, he must be set free for a short time."*

This is the thousand-year period in

which Jesus Christ will reign on the earth, fulfilling God's promises to Abraham and his believing descendants.

This covenant made by God was a literal, eternal and unconditional promise to Abraham that his descendants would one day possess a specific land and that one of his descendants would rule the entire world. The Old Testament prophets anxiously anticipated this earthly reign of the Messiah.

> Isaiah 11:4, 6, 9, NIV: *"⁴ But with righteousness he will judge the needy, with justice he will give decisions for the poor of the earth. He will strike the earth with the rod of his mouth; with the breath of his lips he will slay the wicked. ⁶ The wolf will live with the lamb, the leopard will lie down with the goat, the calf and the lion and the yearling together; and a little child will lead them. ⁹ They will neither harm nor destroy on all my holy mountain, for the earth will be filled with the knowledge of*

the Lord as the waters cover the sea."

It's impossible to place a timeline of these Old Testament prophecies about Christ's rule on the earth in this present age or in eternity. There must be a future time, prior to the new heaven and earth as is described in Revelation 21-22, when God will fulfill these promises to believing Israel. This will be the end of the Millennium.

THE GREAT WHITE
THRONE JUDGMENT

Revelation 20:11-15, NIV: *"¹¹ Then I saw a great white throne and him who was seated on it. The earth and the heavens fled from his presence, and there was no place for them. ¹² And I saw the dead, great and small, standing before the throne, and books were opened. Another book was opened, which is the book of life. The dead were judged according to what they had done as recorded in the books. ¹³ The sea gave* *up the dead that were in it, and death and Hades gave up the dead that were in them, and each person was judged according to what they had done. ¹⁴ Then death and Hades were thrown into the lake of fire. The lake of fire is the second death. ¹⁵ Anyone whose name was not found written in the book of life was thrown into the lake of fire."*

Although only Christians will enter in the Millennium (those unbelievers who survive the Tribulation will be judged at the Second Coming of Christ), there will be people born during the Millennium who will choose to follow Satan instead of Christ.

The Great White Throne Judgment is God's final judgment against all unbelievers who have ever lived.

New Heavens and New Earth

After the Great White Throne Judgment, the present earth will be completely destroyed by fire.

2 Peter 3:7,10, NIV: *"⁷By the same word the present heavens and earth are reserved for fire, being kept for the day of judgment and destruction of the ungodly. ¹⁰But the day of the Lord will come like a thief. The heavens will disappear with a roar; the elements will be destroyed by fire, and the earth and everything done in*

it will be laid bare."

Then, there will be the unveiling of a new heaven and earth.

Revelation 21:1-4, NIV: *"Then I saw 'a new heaven and a new earth,' for the first heaven and the first earth had passed away, and there was no longer any sea. ² I saw the Holy City, the new Jerusalem, coming down out of heaven from God, prepared as a bride beautifully dressed for her husband. ³ And I heard a loud voice from the throne saying, 'Look! God's dwelling place is now among the people, and he will dwell with them. They will be his people, and God himself will be with them and be their God. ⁴ "He will wipe every tear from their eyes. There will be no more death" or mourning or crying or pain, for the old order of things has passed away.'"*

It's important to note the John saw both a new heaven and a new earth. That's important because many Christians have been taught that our eternal home will be in heaven. But later, the Revelator describes earth, not heaven, as our final destination.

And, just as the new heaven and the new earth are the eternal destination of believers, the lake of fire is the permanent destination of unbelievers.

Revelation 20:15, NIV: *"¹⁵ Anyone whose name was not found written in the book of life was thrown into the lake of fire."*

Our trust in the Lord should be strengthened by our understanding of the end times. Because of His salvation plan extended to us, we can escape the reality of hell and experience all that He has in store for us. Understanding the end times should also impact us to live out whatever time we have here on earth in a way that is congruent with Scripture and that pleases God. It should also motivate us to reach out to those who are without Christ.

About Tim R. Barker

Reverend Tim R. Barker is the Superintendent of the South Texas District of the Assemblies of God which is headquartered in Houston, Texas.

He is a graduate of Southwestern Assemblies of God University and received his Doctorate of Ministry Degree from West Coast Seminary.

By virtue of his district office, Reverend Barker is a member of the District's Executive Presbytery; the General

Presbytery of the General Council of the Assemblies of God, Springfield, Missouri; the Executive Board of Regents for Southwestern Assemblies of God University, Waxahachie, Texas; and SAGU-American Indian College, Phoenix, Arizona. He is a member of the Board of Directors of Pleasant Hills Children's Home, Fairfield, Texas, as well as numerous other boards and committees.

Reverend Barker's unique style of pulpit ministry and musical background challenges the body of Christ, with an appeal that reaches the generations.

Contact Tim

Pastor Tim would love to hear from you. You can reach him at www.TimBarker.ag.

Click on Ask Pastor Tim for more information

Made in the USA
Monee, IL
03 June 2020

31928511R00015